POVERTY

Essential Issues

POVERTY

BY MARCIA AMIDON LUSTED

Content Consultant
Buffy Smith, PhD
Department of Sociology
University of St. Thomas, St. Paul, Minnesota

ABDO
Publishing Company

CREDITS

Published by ABDO Publishing Company, 8000 West 78th Street, Edina, Minnesota 55439. Copyright © 2010 by Abdo Consulting Group, Inc. International copyrights reserved in all countries. No part of this book may be reproduced in any form without written permission from the publisher. The Essential Library™ is a trademark and logo of ABDO Publishing Company.

Printed in the United States of America,
North Mankato, Minnesota
102009
012010

PRINTED ON RECYCLED PAPER

Editor: Nadia Higgins
Copy Editor: Rebecca Rowell
Interior Design and Production: Nicole Brecke
Cover Design: Nicole Brecke

Library of Congress Cataloging-in-Publication Data
Lüsted, Marcia Amidon.
  Poverty / Marcia Amidon Lusted.
    p. cm. — (Essential issues)
  Includes bibliographical references.
  ISBN 978-1-60453-957-8
  1. Poverty—Juvenile literature. I. Title.
  HC79.P6.L87 2010
  362.5—dc22

                    2009030333

Poverty

TABLE OF CONTENTS

Janet Mares and her daughter Monica, age nine, pick up groceries at a food bank in California.

WHAT IS POVERTY?

overty has many faces, and it happens everywhere in the world—including the United States. A stranger may not be able to tell that Joan, a 36-year-old white woman, struggles with poverty. Though her story is fictional, it is based on a true story. It serves as an example of one kind of poverty:

Joan's husband has lost his job and is having trouble finding work. Now, Joan is forced to work two low-paying jobs. Even so, the family does not have enough money to make ends meet. They are behind on rent, and their landlord has threatened to evict them from their apartment. These stresses put pressure on the whole family. Joan's teenaged daughter is feeling the effects. She is having trouble sleeping, and her grades are slipping.

Fadmo Muhammed's story is not fictional. She is from Ethiopia and also lives in poverty. She spoke with BBC News:

> I lost one of my children two weeks ago. She died . . . because she was malnourished. We have almost no food. Only donated wheat, and a little oil. But no milk. . . . I am very frightened that my two other children will die as well. They are both sick.[1]

In 2008, 1.4 billion people worldwide lived in extreme poverty. Another 1.9 billion people lived above the poverty line, but they did not make enough money to live comfortably. Almost half the world lived on less than $2.50 per day.

Children at Risk

Poverty has drastic effects on children. They become more vulnerable to being exploited and abused, especially when they are forced into child labor. Children who live in extreme poverty are more likely to perform hazardous jobs—and at the expense of attending school. In 2005, 158 million children—one in six children between the ages of 5 and 14—were working in jobs that were either dangerous or deprived them of an education, according to the United Nations International Children's Emergency Fund (UNICEF).

According to estimates by the U.S. Census Bureau, 12.5 percent of all people lived in poverty in the United States in 2007. Poverty in a drought-stricken village in Africa may look quite different from conditions in an inner-city or a rural community in the United States. However, in both cases, poverty severely limits the ability of people to live successful, healthy lives, with access to health care, education, and good nutrition.

Kinds of Poverty

A person is considered poor if his or her income falls below the poverty line, or poverty level. This is the minimum amount of money an individual requires to meet basic needs. Because the definition of basic needs varies across societies, so does the poverty line. The number of members in a household and their needs also affects the poverty line. This also changes over time.

Poverty has many different causes. A family in Africa may be poor as a result of drought, which has limited its food supplies. Or war may have destroyed

Six-year-old Tariken Lakamu suffers from extreme poverty in Ethiopia.

the family's home and livelihoods or forced its members to become refugees. A family in the United States might live in poverty because of a lack of job opportunities and education. The family members cannot make enough money to meet the U.S. standard of living.

Extreme poverty, which is also referred to as destitution or absolute poverty, is life threatening. It is the lack of even the most basic necessities, such as food, water, housing, and clothing. People in developing countries in Africa, Asia, and Latin America often suffer this type of poverty. In developing regions, extreme poverty is usually defined as earning less than $1.25 a day. In the United States, extreme poverty means earning less than half of the official poverty line.

Relative poverty is when an individual or a family has fewer resources than other people in that same society. In the United States, this usually means a family spends more than a third of its income on food in order to eat adequately. For example, in 2007, the poverty line for a family of four in the United States was $21,203. Though wealthy by African standards, the family would struggle in the United States, where everyday life is more expensive.

Slumdog Millionaire

In 2009, the movie *Slumdog Millionaire* won eight Academy Awards. Set in Mumbai, India, it tells the story of a poor boy who finds himself on the Indian version of the game show *Who Wants to Be a Millionaire?* The movie gives a realistic picture of the poverty and overcrowding in the Mumbai slums. While the movie was filming in Mumbai, one of its child stars had his house bulldozed by the city—a common event in the slums. Producers of the movie found the boy sleeping on a car roof.

Is Poverty Increasing?

Because poverty can be measured many ways, it is often hard to establish how the worldwide rate of poverty is changing. Overall, statistics indicate that the overall percentage of people living in poverty has gone down, falling from 52 percent in 1981 to 26 percent in 2005. However, this decrease has not been equal around the globe. Countries such as China have seen rates go down, while the number of poor people has doubled in Africa.

Another factor affecting worldwide poverty rates is the economic downturn that started in 2008. This

Nickel and Dimed

In 1998, writer Barbara Ehrenreich decided to see what it was like living as a low-wage worker in the United States. She worked a series of jobs, including waitress, house cleaner, and Walmart clerk. She wanted to see if it was possible to find a place to live, buy food, and get by on minimum wage. She discovered that it was not. She shared her experiences in her book *Nickel and Dimed: On (Not) Getting By in America*, writing:

Poverty is acute distress: The lunch that consists of Doritos or hot dog rolls, leading to faintness before the end of the shift. The "home" that is also a car or van. The illness or injury that must be "worked through," with gritted teeth, because there's no sick pay or health insurance and the loss of one day's pay will mean no groceries for the next. These experiences are . . . by almost any standard of subsistence, emergency situations. And that is how we should see the poverty of so many millions of low-wage Americans—as a state of emergency.[2]

The Brandt Line

In 1980, the Brandt Report divided the world in two based on the huge difference in standards of living. The Brandt Line is an imaginary division of the world based on the report. It circles the globe at latitude 30 degrees N, passing between North America and Central America and north of Africa and India. Then, it dips below Australia and New Zealand. Most countries labeled North—those above the line—are developed and wealthy from trade in manufactured goods. Most of the countries labeled South—those below the line—are undeveloped and poor because they do not have extensive trade.

global problem may push many people below the poverty line as unemployment goes up and income levels fall.

WHY DOES POVERTY MATTER?

Poverty limits a person in many ways. It impacts a person's health and his or her prospects for employment and education. Also, the effects of poverty are not limited to those experiencing it. Caring for people living in poverty requires resources from state and national governments, including additional programs in schools and the health-care sector. The general public pays for these programs through taxes.

Civilizations have struggled with the problem of poverty for thousands of years. People have long understood that a successful society manages and assists those who have less. In fact, many of the programs for helping those living in poverty today have their roots in older societies.

A child in Paraguay carries a bag of fruit. His family is among the landless poor who earn low wages farming for wealthy landowners.

*Hammurabi of Babylon, right, codified laws to protect
the poor in approximately 1700 BCE.*

A History of Poverty

Since the beginning of recorded history, poverty has caused sharp differences between the rich and the poor. A few civilizations developed their own rules and methods for dealing with the poor. In other civilizations, the rich often mistreated the poor.

In some civilizations, classes clearly separated the rich and the poor. Widows, orphans, and prisoners of war were generally in the lowest class. Other early civilizations were based more on agriculture—they produced just enough food for survival. These societies were less likely to have a stark division between rich and poor, and one's social position was usually based on family ties, not wealth.

The Code of Hammurabi

Writings from ancient civilizations show that they often tried to deal fairly with the poor. In approximately 1700 BCE, King Hammurabi ruled the Mesopotamian city of Babylon, in present-day Iraq. He established a set of laws known as the Code of Hammurabi that addressed the treatment of the different classes. For example, one law outlined debt repayment. It put a time limit on how long people in debt could perform forced labor as a way to fulfill their loans. In this way, they were protected from becoming lifelong slaves.

The Code of Hammurabi set laws in writing—they could not be changed or interpreted on a whim. It outlined relationships between the rich and the poor in everyday life. Punishments were based on the class of the person, but they were fair. Other writings, such as those of early Christians and Jews, took another approach. They urged wealthy people to help the poor because it was the morally right thing to do.

The Poor Laws

Beginning in the late sixteenth century, Great Britain developed a new idea about poverty—the poor could not help being poor. As such, society had a duty to help them maintain a basic standard of living. The so-called Poor Laws, which were established and modified by Great Britain from the late sixteenth century until 1948, reflected this attitude.

A Poor Law from 1601 enumerated several practices for helping the poor that would be funded by a property tax. For example, any children whose own families could not support them would be sent to live with other families. The law also set up conditions for able-bodied poor people to work, supported people who were unable to work, and encouraged children to learn trades.

The Poor Laws became the basis for many modern welfare programs, which began in the

United States in the 1930s. However, in the 1970s and 1980s, a shift occurred in attitudes toward the poor in the United States. With the expansion of the economy and plenty of jobs, people began to view unemployment as the individual's own choice. With so many jobs available, they argued, any able-bodied person should be able to get a decent job. This attitude persists though many fully employed people still cannot make ends meet.

Colonization and Poverty

Beginning in approximately 1450, European explorers had begun sailing all over the globe in search of wealth. They encountered many thriving cultures that were rich in natural resources. They began to take over these societies. The Europeans turned them into colonies, helping themselves to the native people's gold, silver, cotton, rubber, and sugar. As European nations became industrialized starting in the early nineteenth century, their need

"The Magnificent African Cake"

In 1884, slavery had ended in Africa, but Europeans were greedily eyeing the continent as a place to colonize. The result was the "scramble for Africa," with each European country scrambling to get as much land as it could. In 1884, the European countries divided Africa as if they were slicing a cake, giving themselves each a portion. King Leopold II of Belgium called Africa a "magnificent African cake."[1] He then established the Congo Free State with his "slice," which basically became his own private estate.

for those raw materials increased—Earth's resources
fueled their factories. European countries used their
sophisticated weapons to take over African and Asian
countries by force. By 1914, almost 90 percent of
the world was controlled by countries in the West—
European nations and those in North America that
had been founded by European settlers.

The West reaped great wealth, while the natives
who lived in colonies became poorer and poorer.
Their bad situation was double-edged: not only did
they often suffer from terrible working conditions,
their ability to grow their own food was often taken
away as well. For example, colonizers took land away
from local farmers. Then, instead of growing food,
colonizers used the land to grow cash crops such as
cotton for export. In this way, colonization led to an
unequal distribution of wealth and natural resources
throughout the world, dividing it into the rich and
the poor.

The Price of Industrialization

Meanwhile, beginning in the mid-nineteenth
century, the Industrial Revolution increased poverty
in Europe and North America. New factories and
machines that produced more goods faster brought

greater profits to the factory owners. However, the workers did not share in the wealth that their hours of hard labor helped create.

Many people left their rural homes to travel to cities and work in the factories. By leaving their farms, they were no longer self-sufficient. They could no longer produce their own food and clothing without the need for actual cash. Now, the workers had to rely on their wages to purchase what they needed to survive. If these workers lost their jobs or became

The Great Depression

In the 1930s, the United States faced severe economic problems during the Great Depression. Unemployment skyrocketed, and farm production slumped. Before then, the country had relied on private charities to care for the poor. As the Depression worsened, organizations such as the Red Cross sent out food baskets and set up soup kitchens. However, they could not keep up with the tremendous demand.

President Herbert Hoover opposed giving government money directly to the poor. He believed that businesses would eventually recover by themselves. His administration's policy was to make state and city governments responsible for providing relief efforts for their citizens—but these local governments did not have the funds to do so.

It took a new president, Franklin Delano Roosevelt, to address the problem. Elected in 1932, Roosevelt transformed the role of government in shaping the nation's economy. Under his New Deal, the government provided direct relief to the poor. It employed thousands through work programs and reformed banking and businesses. Roosevelt also established policies such as Social Security, which attempts to reduce poverty among the elderly, and welfare.

sick and could not work, they lost their wages and fell into poverty. The overpowering need to make enough money to support a family forced parents to send their children to work in factories as well. The children often labored in dangerous jobs and for long hours.

The Industrial Revolution created the working class, the people who had to work for wages—often doing manual labor—in order to survive. This class was likely to live in poverty, while wealthy factory owners no longer had to actually work. Members of the upper class were well educated, and this allowed them to remain in the top tier of society. But poverty for the working class was self-perpetuating. They rarely had the chance to become educated and so often remained in poverty for their entire lives.

Today, the effects of the past linger. Modern poverty exists partly because of the conditions set in motion throughout history. However, poverty is also fueled by current problems, including war, environmental conditions, and economic depressions.

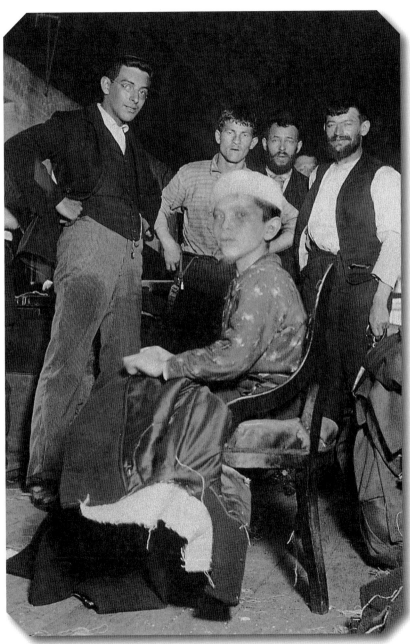

In the early twentieth century, workers take a break from making clothes in a New York City sweatshop.

Victoriano Lemus, a migrant worker, holds his son outside their mobile home in California.

POVERTY TODAY

In June 2007, the *Detroit News* published an article about Keiara Bell, a teenager who lived in poverty. Keiara's father was disabled and out of work. Though he received a monthly check from Social Security, the meager earnings could not support the family. To make ends meet, Keiara's father and mother sold candy from the trunk of their car, a secondhand taxi. The nickels and dimes they earned helped them scrape together enough to buy items such as gas and milk. "I'm tired of . . . living like this," Keiara said, though no end to the situation was in sight.[1] As her father said, "There's nothing. No money. No job. No prospect of a job. It boils up and you want to explode."[2]

Keiara and her family lived in Detroit, Michigan. In 2007, Detroit was the poorest large city in the country, with 33.8 percent of its population in poverty. At the time, the government's poverty line for families was $21,203 a year.

Keiara's experience evokes images and ideas that most people associate with poverty in the United States today: inner cities with burned buildings, vacant lots, soaring high school drop-out rates, and out-of-control crime. But other types of poverty exist in the nation.

Recessions and Poverty

A recession is a downturn in the economy marked by job losses and lower housing values. Recessions affect all citizens, but they hit those already living at or near poverty the hardest, especially children. As prices increase and families have less money or lose their jobs, those with children to support are most likely to fall into poverty. Based on past recessions, it is projected that the recession that began in 2008 will have the same effect.

Rural Poverty

Many rural places in the United States have been poverty-stricken for decades, including Appalachia, American Indian reservations in the Southwest and Midwest, and the Mississippi Delta region in the South. Poor employment opportunities and low education levels plague these regions. These factors make it almost impossible for the poor people who live there to escape from poverty.

Rural areas present additional challenges to the poor. Remote areas are isolated from the kinds of social services that cities might be able to provide for the poor. They also

Poverty, Inc.

In 1980, Hartford, Connecticut, was a booming city. New condominiums, restaurants, and other services for the middle class filled the downtown area. But by 1990, the city's population began to shrink as more and more families moved to the suburbs. Restaurants and hotels in downtown Hartford closed, and some of the city's biggest employers closed or relocated. Of those people who still lived in the city proper, approximately 25 percent were on welfare. Hartford became known for its willingness to provide programs to help the poor, earning it the nickname "Poverty, Inc."

In 2009, Hartford had an unemployment rate of 6.7 percent, which was lower than the national average. However, the city's rate of child poverty was 47 percent. Surveys also showed that 41 percent of the adult population in the Greater Hartford area was functioning below a sufficient level of literacy. They would not be able to get living-wage jobs. Hartford is a good illustration of how difficult it can be to overcome poverty in the city.

lack public transportation that would enable those without cars to get to jobs.

Another group that suffers from rural poverty consists of migrant workers, who earn their livings harvesting crops such as strawberries, grapes, and potatoes. They travel from crop to crop, all over the country, working 10 to 12 hours a day. Migrant workers make so little money that they cannot afford adequate housing. Instead, they often must crowd together in tiny, unheated rooms or garages.

Migrant workers are particularly ill-treated because competition in the agricultural industry is so fierce. The pressure makes employers resort to ruthless measures to keep costs as low as possible. Growers have been known to go so far as to make workers pay for the tools they use or the water they drink on the job.

A Different Degree of Poverty

Absolute poverty is so extreme that even the poorest U.S. citizen might seem much better off in comparison. A 2009 story on National Public Radio described the lives of people in South Africa who were forced to make a living selling other people's garbage:

*In Manila, a city in the Philippines, scavengers sift
through garbage looking for food.*

*The beeping sound of a garbage truck dumping its load serves
as the dinner bell for people like Katie Scholtz and her partner,
George Richan. Sometimes an unfinished lunch discarded by
a schoolchild serves as a meal for the couple, who live in the
bush near the dump. Richan also scavenges for broken radios,
which he either repairs or recycles by selling the copper wires
within. The money he makes from the tossed radios is used to
buy food. More than a dozen men and women scavenge [in
the dump], searching through the putrid waste.[3]*

Like other forms of poverty, absolute poverty
makes its victims society's least powerful members.

But this level of poverty also leads to a level of desperation shown by these scavengers in South Africa.

TRANSITIONAL COUNTRIES

Poverty also exists in "transitional" countries, such as those that belonged to the former Soviet Union and are now self-governing. Since the fall of the Soviet Union in 1989, the poverty level in many countries in Eastern Europe and Central Asia has increased. In 2004, reporter John Schenk described the experience of a poor family in Kosovo, a country in Eastern Europe where 62 percent of the population lived in poverty:

Poverty in Darfur

Since 2003, the African region of Darfur has been devastated by conflicts, which have been closely tied to the causes of poverty. Darfur has been harmed by desertification. As more land becomes unsuitable for farming, more people are vying with each other for the limited resource. This has led to wars between tribes, which have led to widespread famine and genocide. More than 300,000 people have died in Darfur since the conflicts began, and 2.6 million are homeless.

Six children in the Budakova family share four pairs of boots. There are three shifts at their village school, so the children rotate the best clothing and the limited pairs of footwear in the household to whomever is headed for class. [The family lives] on significantly less than $1 per person per day.[4]

Transitional countries in Eastern Europe used to follow communism, in which the government owned businesses, factories, and farms. The goal of communism was to provide equality and economic security to all citizens—though the reality strayed far from this ideal. Many people under communist regimes were poorer than people who lived in democracies. However, they were not destitute. Communism ensured that their basic needs were met.

With the collapse of the Soviet Union, many celebrated the fall of communism in Eastern Europe. They hoped for democracy and better economies for the countries formerly under Soviet control. Instead, many countries suffered from economic and political conflicts. These problems devalued their currencies, making the average person's money worth much less in the marketplace. Services such as free health care were also frequently disrupted or dissolved. Wars, such as those involving Bosnia and Herzegovina in 1991, often led to ethnic cleansings. Many members of particular ethnic groups were killed. Others fled their homes only to become poverty-stricken refugees in other countries.

*In Romania, a woman makes ends meet by selling produce on the streets.
In a phone booth, she finds shelter from the rain.*

Farmers in Myanmar work the fields by hand. Subsistence farming methods contribute to poverty in developing nations.

THE UNDERLYING CAUSES

The economy takes a downturn, and job opportunities dry up. A family's main earner falls ill, and they cannot pay their medical bills. Drought strikes a village in Africa, and crops fail. War forces people from their homes. Lack of trade limits economic opportunities in a developing nation. Laborers with no way out are forced to work for a pittance in sweatshops and farms. Racism denies opportunities to minority groups. There are so many ways to become—and to remain— poor.

Poverty in Developing Countries

One of the most basic causes of poverty is overpopulation, or having too many people in a limited space. With too few resources to share, people cannot survive simply by farming, herding, or hunting and gathering. Poverty based in overpopulation most often occurs in developing countries, where people count on subsistence farming to feed themselves. Farmers rely on manual labor, which does not yield large amounts of food. So, even large areas of land can support only a small number of people, and many go hungry.

In Africa, many are living in poverty as a result of the AIDS epidemic that has swept through the continent. The disease has deprived families of income-earning adults while saddling the survivors with medical and funeral expenses.

Natural Disasters and Poverty

People who live in poorer countries are more likely to die from natural disasters than those in wealthier countries. Countries such as the United States, Canada, and Japan can withstand disasters and diseases better than poor countries because they have more resources. For example, they can build and maintain strong buildings that withstand earthquakes. Their medical facilities and sophisticated emergency response systems save lives after disaster strikes.

People who belong to racial and ethnic minorities also find themselves in poverty because of prejudice, which deprives them of fair treatment and employment opportunities. An extreme and well-known example of crippling prejudice was the apartheid system in South Africa. *Apartheid* means "separateness," and under this rigid system of segregation, people of color were oppressed. For example, their rights to own property were severely limited. Apartheid ended in 1991, but many South African blacks remain in extreme poverty.

Environmental problems also contribute to poverty in developing countries. Issues such as climate change and drought harm crops. This simultaneously raises food prices while limiting people's ability to grow their own food. Another factor is soil erosion caused by efforts to eke out crops on overused land. The rich soil has been robbed of nutrients, making it unsuitable for farming.

Wars and other armed conflicts also contribute to poverty by destroying houses, farmland, and businesses. They also limit or end access to health care. Families in war-torn areas may flee their homes seeking safety. They become refugees in other countries, with no money or means of support. If they do not speak the language of their new country, refugees may have extreme difficulty finding work.

A CHANCE TO LEARN

In several poor countries, many people cannot read or write and have never attended school. Without education, they cannot find sustaining work. Sulemana Alhassan, 13, lives in Ghana, a country in Africa. He does not go to school but works instead selling water on the streets:

> *Sulemana's day begins as early as 5:30 a.m., and he carts water back and forth until 1 p.m. Sometimes, to keep up with the customers' demands, he starts again at 4 p.m. All the money he and his brother earn goes to their father, who uses it to buy food. Even though Sulemana says he wants to be in school instead of fetching water every day, he seems resigned to his fate.* [1]

In poor countries, the governments cannot afford to provide good schools. Even when schooling is available, poor families may not send their children because they need the children to work instead.

ONE FOR YOU, TWO FOR ME

Another cause of poverty in developing nations is the unequal distribution of resources. On a global scale, the world's richest 20 percent of the population consumes 76.6 percent of the world's resources. At the same time, the poorest 20 percent of the world's people consume only 1.5 percent of its resources. According to the organization Share the World's

Spending Priorities

Almost half of the world lives on less than $2.50 a day, and many people cannot buy the basic necessities to survive. And yet in many developed countries, the amount of money spent on luxury items is sobering. In the United States every year, $8 billion is spent on cosmetics. And in both Europe and the United States, $12 billion is spent on perfumes and $17 billion on pet food. Around the world, $400 billion is spent on illegal drugs. That is a total of $437 billion.

What would it cost to meet basic human needs for everyone in the world? Basic education for everyone would cost $6 billion. Water and sanitation would cost $9 billion. Reproductive health for all women would cost $12 billion, and basic health and nutrition for every single person in the world would be $13 billion. That is a total of $40 billion—a fraction of what the world spends on luxury items and illegal drugs.

Resources, "More than 1.4 billion people live in poverty so extreme that they can barely survive . . . whilst a new billionaire is created every second day."[2]

Some of this global inequality of resources developed from the colonization period, when richer industrialized countries deprived smaller ones of their natural resources and their ability to build strong economies. Even after they gained independence, the smaller countries were often unable to compete in the global economy.

POOR IN A WEALTHY SOCIETY

A person who lives in poverty in the United States enjoys a standard of living that would seem high to someone in a developing country. But, in a developed country, expectations are higher. In the United States, for example, living without indoor plumbing and heat is considered an extreme hardship. In a developing country, a family might be considered well-off if they have a garden big enough to feed their family, some livestock, and a mud-brick house.

Also, in developed countries basic goods cost more. People with minimum-wage jobs may not be able to afford even housing and food, let alone

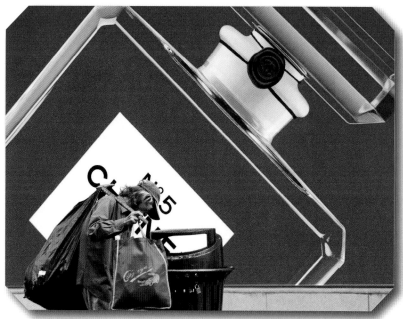

*In Shanghai, China, a scavenger looks through the trash.
Behind him is an advertisement for perfume.*

items such as cars or toys for their children. They may require government assistance simply to get by. Adding to their difficulty is the constant tension between the "haves" and "have-nots." In a society saturated with advertising, it may seem to poor people that everyone else has everything they want.

CAUSES OF POVERTY IN DEVELOPED NATIONS

Changing trends in a country's economy can cause relative poverty. In weak economic times, such as what the United States began experiencing in 2008, jobs become more difficult to obtain.

Lack of education is also a problem in developed countries. Without a college degree, an individual may have difficulty finding a well-paying job. He or she will likely get stuck in minimum-wage jobs.

The divorce rate is another factor. A high divorce rate results in more single-parent families, which are usually poorer than two-parent homes with two incomes. Single mothers in particular are especially vulnerable, resulting in a trend known as the "feminization of poverty." These mothers tend to face unique financial challenges: child care expenses, an inability to earn as much as a man does in most jobs, and frequent difficulties collecting child support payments from their ex-husbands.

Born to Be Poor?

In developed nations, some people are born into a culture of poverty, where being poor is considered normal. Some experts argue those born into poverty may not aspire to rise out of it because

Dropping Out

Studies have shown that kids who drop out of high school are more likely to have low skill levels and ultimately end up living in poverty and requiring government assistance. High school dropouts usually stay on government assistance longer than those who have completed high school. They are also more likely to become involved in criminal activity.

it is the only life example they have. Experts have identified traits that characterize those who live in a culture of poverty. A person in this situation is constantly struggling for money. If he is employed, his job is likely menial and low paying. His family does not keep groceries in the home. Instead, they buy food as they need it throughout the day. To get cash, he is likely to pawn personal items or borrow money from lenders who charge high interest rates. The result is large debt, which sinks him even further into poverty.

The Gender Gap

No matter whether the overall economy is healthy or weak, women are more likely than men to be poor, and the poverty rate for single mothers is three times higher than the overall poverty rate. According to Erica Williams of the Institute for Women's Policy Research, "Being female continues to jeopardize one's economic security, and being a mother creates an additional economic disadvantage."[3]

In developed countries, some people say generous welfare policies perpetuate cycles of poverty. They argue that welfare payments motivate recipients to stay poor in order to keep receiving aid. However, the main U.S. welfare program, known as Temporary Assistance for Needy Families, has a limit of five years, after which most families can no longer receive benefits. Also, workfare programs require welfare recipients to be actively seeking employment.

*Children play outside a housing complex for poor families
in Cleveland, Ohio.*

*Neil Floyd, a homeless man in Camden, New Jersey,
starts a fire to keep warm in the snow.*

HOMELESSNESS

omelessness is a very real and often dangerous effect of poverty. It can even be fatal. In 2003, a 50-year-old homeless man was found dead in Detroit, Michigan. Exposed to the elements, he had frozen to death:

A neighborhood resident found his body under a large cardboard box in an alley. He had attempted to create a shelter under the box, using blankets as walls. He was the second homeless person to have frozen to death in Detroit [that] winter.[1]

Who Is Homeless?

A homeless person may be someone who cannot afford to live in a house or an apartment. But homelessness includes people whose primary residence is a homeless shelter, an institution, a car, or a public place not meant to be lived in, such as a mall, a bus station, or a street. Homeless people include entire families, individuals who are temporarily without a place to live, and people with mental disorders who cannot afford their treatments and have nowhere to go.

Even employed people can become homeless. According to the National Coalition for the Homeless, "Many homeless people do not make enough money to pay rent even if they work every single day. Some homeless people even work two minimum wage jobs and still do not have enough money to afford rent."[2]

HOUSING PROBLEMS

The primary cause of U.S. homelessness is the skyrocketing cost of renting an apartment or buying or building a home, coupled with a lack of work opportunities. Renting poses particular difficulties. Most landlords require a security deposit and the first month's rent in advance. A renter may have to put down a thousand dollars or more before even moving in. So, even if someone working a low-paying job could afford the monthly rent on an apartment, he or she probably would not be able to come up with the initial sum needed to secure it.

Homelessness and the Recession

The number of people who find themselves homeless increases during a recession. As more people lose their jobs and are unable to afford mortgage payments or rent, charities and local government programs are overwhelmed with requests for assistance. They are forced to turn needy people away.

The mortgage crisis that began in 2008 resulted in the foreclosure of thousands of homes. Many people who were not qualified to receive a home loan were able to buy houses that were beyond their means. They did so through subprime mortgages with low interest rates. When the rates rose and the payments increased, these people were unable to pay their mortgages.

Such a crisis affects renters when their landlords default on mortgages and lose their properties. Through no fault of their own, the renters are forced out of their homes. In 2008, the National Alliance to End Homelessness estimated that approximately 866,000 more Americans would experience homelessness in 2009 and 2010. Many homeless shelters could not keep up with the numbers of people appearing on their doorsteps.

Also, rent is only one of many bills, including food, child care, health care, and education. Poor people may need to make difficult choices about which bills to pay—and which ones not to pay. Because housing is so expensive, it may be the cost to drop. As the National Coalition for the Homeless pointed out, "Being poor means being an illness, an accident, or a paycheck away from living on the streets."[3]

For workers who do not own a car, homelessness may also result from a lack of affordable housing close to their workplaces. Even in cities with a public transportation system, the operating hours of the transit system may not fit well with the individual's working hours.

In addition, many cities lack affordable housing. The amount of affordable housing available in a community depends on several factors. The population of an area, and whether it is increasing or decreasing, is one factor. Another is whether governmental controls exist on the cost of rent. Other factors are if the neighborhood itself is improving or declining and how much new housing is being created.

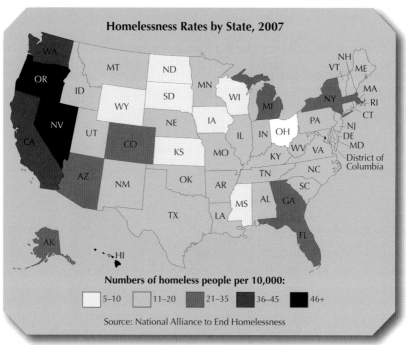

Hawaii, Oregon, Nevada, and Washington DC
have the highest rates of homelessness.

In some cities, gentrification is a problem.
This happens when formerly affordable housing
is renovated into expensive condominiums for the
wealthy, or it is demolished to make way for new
business development. Either way, the result is a lack
of affordable housing. The National Coalition for
the Homeless reports that 2.2 million low-rent units
disappeared from the housing market between 1973
and 1993, mostly because they became unaffordable.

Rural areas may also suffer from a shortage of affordable housing. Some communities have strict zoning laws that hamper new construction or price it out of reach. For example, a town's zoning laws may require large lots for single-family homes. To preserve the town's appeal, laws also regulate the appearance of homes. Meanwhile, people with limited means cannot afford the price of the land, let alone the cost of a house.

COPING STRATEGIES

Writer Bea Sheftel asks what you would do if you were faced with homelessness. She writes:

> *What if you had a good job but were living just above your means? And then you were laid off and couldn't pay the rent on your apartment? What would you do? Would you be too proud to go to a homeless shelter? Afraid to mingle with people at the shelter?*[4]

Those who lose their homes have few options. They may start by moving in with family or friends, maybe sleeping on their couches or floors. Others may live in cheap hotel rooms that cater to people in their situations, living alone or splitting the rent with others.

Who Pays for Shelters?

Local, state, or national governments can fund homeless shelters. Many are also run by religious organizations or charitable groups and rely on public contributions and volunteer labor. The U.S. Department of Housing and Urban Development also provides emergency shelter grants to rehabilitate or convert existing buildings into shelters.

Still others move into their cars, parking their vehicles in business or church parking lots. They use bathrooms in public places, perhaps showering in college gyms. Often referred to as "auto tramps," they are everywhere.

The last stop for the homeless, after all other possibilities have been exhausted, is the street. Some live in shelters, and some spend their days in warm places such as Laundromats and libraries. Others live completely on the streets, sleeping in cardboard boxes, ramshackle homemade shelters, or doorways.

THE DANGERS

Homelessness can have many negative effects. In cold climates, winter can be dangerous to homeless people without sufficient shelter—they can even die from exposure. Also, homeless people have a limited ability to wash and change clothes. As a result, they may have trouble getting jobs because they do not appear employable. Lack of a telephone number, Internet access, and other communication technologies may also make it difficult to find a job. Limited access to banks makes it difficult to save money because most bank accounts require proof of residency. Homelessness also results in discrimination because the general public associates the problem with substance abuse or mental illness.

Homeless people are also more often victims of violent crimes. Women who live on the streets are especially vulnerable to sexual abuse and rape. Many of them neglect personal hygiene or bundle up in many layers on purpose in order to discourage sexual predators.

Because homeless people have reduced access to health care, many suffer ailments that would be easily treatable with consistent medical care. Others may suffer from mental illnesses that could be controlled with medicine or other treatments. The number of people suffering from schizophrenia, bipolar disorder, and personality disorders is abnormally high among the homeless. They are also less likely to receive proper care because they have trouble

Portable Shelters

Every large city struggles with the question of how to shelter its homeless population. Contemporary architects are experimenting with designs for portable personal shelters that could be erected quickly and easily, protect the inhabitant from cold and precipitation, and be economical. Most of the experimental designs resemble single-person inflatable tents or oversized sleeping bags.

Homeless Teens

Teens may be homeless because their families are homeless, or they may not have a residence because they have run away or been kicked out of their homes. Some are referred to as "couch hoppers" because they spend a few weeks at a friend's or a relative's house and then move to another house, concealing their home-lessness. Others live in shelters or on the streets. Homeless teens often have difficulties in school. This is compounded by the fact that they may resist seeking the help they need because they want to keep their home-lessness a secret.

getting to treatment centers, forget appointments and medications, and may be unruly or unresponsive because of drug abuse.

Homeless children are less likely to receive adequate education because they may move frequently or not attend school at all. They have limited access to the kinds of support systems that would help them with school. They also may suffer from developmental delays because of past traumas, and the stress of their daily lives can lead to emotional and behavioral problems. Homeless children also have a higher risk for health problems, such as asthma and lead poisoning, as well as infectious diseases.

Tabitha Velazquez and her son relax at an outreach center for homeless kids and teens in San Diego, California.

Tenth-grade teacher Stacey Vore prepares breakfast for low-income students in Lorain, Ohio.

POVERTY AND EDUCATION

One aspect of poverty, in particular, often leads to a vicious cycle of generational poverty. This is poverty's effect on the ability of children and teenagers to receive a good education. Receiving a high-quality education, from a high school diploma to a college degree, is one way to escape the cycle of poverty because it helps people obtain jobs that pay more than minimum wage. But people living in poverty have fewer resources when it comes to education. They also have fewer support systems to make them want to become well educated. Finally, they often attend inferior schools in poor areas. If they grow up in a culture that is not educated and does not value education, poor children and teenagers often face extreme difficulty breaking out of the cycle. Otis is an elementary school student with many disadvantages. His story shows how his mother's lack of education limits his own:

> *Otis comes home from school and announces that the school is going to have a reading contest. For every five books his mother reads to him, he will receive a coupon to get $5 off a pizza. To obtain his books, he needs his mother to go to the library. She isn't sure she can even read to him because her skills were never very good, and she hasn't read for a long time. Getting to the library requires them to walk because they don't have a car. There were two drive-by shootings last week. He also tells his mom that the school is having an open house and is sending a bus around the neighborhood to pick up parents. He gives his mom a note that she can't read.[1]*

The Value of Education

Compare Otis's story to Katie's. A typical third-grader living in a middle-class suburb, Katie comes home from school with a project to do that involves making a map of Africa. She immediately turns on her family's computer and uses the Internet to research Africa. Then, she retrieves an atlas from her family's bookshelf and finds the information she needs to make her map. Katie's mother or father then helps her assemble the materials she needs—even if it means an extra trip to the store. They guide her as she does the project, and then they help her get it to school the next day. Katie's parents, who are both college-educated, know how important education is. They make sure that Katie also realizes how important it is to do her homework and get good grades.

Katie's scenario may sound familiar to many kids, but for kids living in poverty, it might as well be a scene from a television show. Otis's mother may have wanted to help Otis, but she did not have the time, money, or skills to help him. Her own poor education was now limiting his. According to William Bainbridge in an article in the *Columbus Dispatch*:

[The most relevant factors] in predicting academic achievement are family socioeconomics and the education levels of the students' parents (and of other adults close to them). The best predictor of a child's success in school is the education level of the parents, particularly the mother.[2]

OBSTACLES TO SUCCESS BEGAN EARLY

Children from low-income homes have other disadvantages, too. Even in the womb, poor children may have lacked necessary prenatal care from their mothers, who did not have access to good medical care. Poor children may have watched too much television in their first years of life. Or they may not have received enough attention at home from exhausted, overworked parents. Limited access to preschool programs may have deprived them of early childhood education opportunities as well. All of these factors could have limited the development of their growing brains.

Poverty and Children's Brains

Living in poverty not only affects a child's ability to receive a good education, it may also affect his or her brain function. Studies comparing wealthy nine- or ten-year-old children to their low-income peers show that brain function in the poor children is markedly lower. Factors such as malnutrition, stress, and illiterate environments may cause poor children's neural systems to develop differently. As a result, their language development is affected, as are their abilities to plan, remember details, and pay attention in school.

At a Back-to-School Giveaway in Los Angeles, California, needy students receive backpacks full of school supplies.

Language development is also slowed. Studies have shown that children in poor families are exposed to fewer words and, as a result, use fewer words. Their average vocabulary is 800 words, compared to vocabularies of 1,200 to 1,300 words of other children the same age.

GETTING THERE IS HALF THE BATTLE

Poverty may affect the child's ability to even get to school in the morning and to stay enrolled in the same school throughout the year. Poor families may be forced to relocate frequently to find better employment. They may move because they have been evicted or their water or electricity has been turned off because of unpaid bills. This forces the child to change schools, which is disruptive.

Kids who move frequently are considered to be those who have moved more than once in the past two years or three or more times in the past five years. With each move, they have to make new friends, and they miss important lessons. In fact, it is estimated that a student loses three to six months of education with each transition. It comes as no surprise, then, that students who frequently change schools are more likely than their peers to repeat a grade. Later, they are more likely to drop out of school.

Schools have difficulty helping these children, as teachers have trouble assessing their needs. They may not know enough about the kids' past education or what is missing from their learning.

Good Schools and Not-So-Good Schools

Kids living in poverty are also at a disadvantage because of the low quality of the schools in their low-income neighborhoods. Kids in middle-class towns and suburbs usually attend schools that are funded reasonably well. Their parents and the taxpayers who pay for these schools believe in the value of a good education—and they have enough money to promote this value. These schools are more likely to have high-quality equipment, computers, and books. Even more important, these schools attract good teachers. The end result is a quality education that will enable students to attend college and go on to find good jobs.

Underfunded schools in inner cities or extreme rural areas, however, may lack even the basics.

Teacher Training

Many teachers now attend workshops about how, specifically, living in poverty may affect a child's behavior and academic performance. In many areas, the number of students from low-income families is increasing every year. Teachers need to know how best to teach these children to achieve maximum success in school.

Teachers might need to adjust their teaching strategies to compensate for children who use different methods of gathering information, need more structure and clearer instructions about how to accomplish tasks, and may not have the same vocabulary as their peers. Children from unpredictable environments might need help learning to plan and predict cause-and-effect situations as well as controlling impulsive behavior. They also may need learning situations that are more hands-on and less instructive, such as learning math through measuring, creating a woodworking project, or rewriting a story to tell it in their own words and style of speaking.

Many schools are funded by property taxes, which are taxes on the value of people's homes in the community. In low-income areas, homes may not be worth much, or the majority of people may not even own homes. That makes property taxes—and school funding—low.

These schools may not have libraries, playgrounds, or enrichment classes such as art or music. They may lack programs for special education or students who do not speak English. They are also less likely to have up-to-date computers and other technologies.

Because salaries at the school are not competitive, it may not be able to attract talented teachers. And current teachers often feel overworked and stressed. This is partly because students in poor schools, who have moved frequently or do not come from stable homes, tend to have more behavioral problems.

Comparing Schools

Schools with wealthier populations have more money for extra programs and equipment, more up-to-date technology, and additional enrichment activities for their students. Their facilities may be new or well maintained. Poorly funded schools are often deteriorating buildings where basics such as heat and water may be in short supply, books are old and out-of-date, and technology is old or nonexistent. Poor high schools may not be accredited, which means they have not met the national standards that ensure a minimum quality of education. That may make acceptance by good colleges harder for students from these schools.

Teachers' energy and time is sapped dealing with these problems. They may feel they have neither the financial support nor emotional support to get through the day.

Finally, city schools may be located in high crime areas. Students in such areas are more likely to be involved in crime than in other areas. That can make school feel unsafe, which is a major disruption to learning in conditions that are already less than ideal.

In Sacramento, California, a school official denounces cuts to education funding in 2008. Nearby, two first-graders also express their opinions.

*Silvia Esquivias, 24, exits a mobile health clinic after receiving
a free exam in central Pennsylvania.*

POVERTY AND HEALTH

No matter where you live in the world,
being poor is bad for your health. It is
a vicious cycle. Without education, it is difficult to
get a job with health care benefits. But it is more
difficult for poor children to do well in school and

ultimately get jobs that will provide health care insurance. SueAnn's story shows how poor health care is harming her daughter's education:

> SueAnn's daughter is 15 and pregnant. [SueAnn] needs $400 to pay the doctor so that he will keep seeing her [daughter]. SueAnn has told her [daughter] she needs to go to the clinic where the service is free. However, the wait is usually three to four hours, and she misses half a day of school. There is also the problem of getting her there. It's in a bad part of town, and it will be dark before SueAnn can get there to pick her up.[1]

Behind from the Start

Children born in poverty begin their lives at a disadvantage. With a lack of health insurance, most pregnant women living in poverty will not have proper prenatal care. These pregnant women may also suffer from high blood pressure, diabetes, or other medical conditions that might put their babies at risk for premature birth. Infant mortality rates are higher than average among the poor.

Children growing up in poverty also suffer from poor diets. Fresh fruits and vegetables are expensive, and most poor families cannot afford to eat enough

Malnutrition

According to UNICEF, malnutrition is a silent emergency around the globe, killing millions of people every year and keeping countries from being economically successful. Malnutrition can also cause long-lasting damage to health in those who survive. For example, an iodine deficiency can cause brain damage. Malnutrition can result in stunted growth, and its effects span generations. Malnourished girls can grow up to give birth to malnourished children.

of these healthful foods. They may eat fast food or other cheap, convenient foods that are fatty or fried, low in nutrients, high in sugar and salt, and starchy. The combination of a poor diet and a lack of health care puts poor children at risk for long-term problems such as obesity, heart disease, and asthma.

An Unhealthy Environment

People who live in poverty are also at risk because of where they live. Homeless people or those who live in substandard housing may suffer more ill health simply because of exposure to the elements. Inadequate shelter may bring a greater risk of disease borne by insects or rodents, especially in developing countries. Occupants of houses without proper heat—or in warm climates, air-conditioning—have a greater risk of illnesses caused by extreme temperatures. And they may already be susceptible to such illness because they have not had proper health care or nutrition on a regular basis.

Thurman Yazzie lives in a trailer with no power or running water in Arizona. He waits for his mother to finish cooking dinner outside.

Poor sanitation, such as the lack of running water and sewage systems, also contributes to the potential for illness. Open sewage and garbage dumps attract disease-carrying vermin. Crowded conditions, such as in shantytowns, make it easier for airborne diseases to be transmitted from person to person.

Lead paint poses another environmental health hazard to poor children. Older houses and apartments that have not been properly maintained may harbor lead paint, paint chips, and dust, which can be inhaled or even consumed by the children who live there. Children may get lead dust on their fingers and then put them in their mouths, or they may put objects with lead paint in their mouths. Lead poisoning can be very harmful. It can delay a child's physical and mental development, causing low intelligence levels, short attention spans, and behavioral problems.

Losing Welfare, Losing Health Care

It may seem that getting people off welfare and putting them into jobs can only be a positive step. However, in many cases, this move means that those who formerly received subsidized health care from the government now find themselves uninsured. Many employers either do not offer health care for their employees, or health care coverage requires a waiting period of several months before the employee can enroll. People who work in part-time jobs are often not eligible for health care at all.

Even when an employee is eligible to receive health care, the premiums often simply cost too much. This is especially true for those who work in retail. In that case, health care might cost $1.50 of a $10 hourly wage. As a result, many working families end up without any health care at all, and they become more vulnerable to illnesses and injuries that may make it difficult for them to maintain their jobs. This is just one of many reasons why it is so difficult for families to leave the welfare system.

No Time to Be Sick

People living in poverty usually need to work no matter what—even when they are sick. Because they work low-paying jobs, they usually do not receive paid sick leave. Or, if they work more than one job, they may not be able to take a sick day from both.

They are forced to work even when they are sick or injured, increasing the likelihood that their conditions will be prolonged or become worse.

The inability to get to a doctor or a clinic compounds the problem. Without health insurance, most poor people rely on free health care from government-subsidized clinics or other free or low-cost facilities. These facilities may be inaccessible by public transportation. If a family does not have a car or has very little money for gas, a trip to the clinic on the other side of town may be out of the question. As a result, illnesses and injuries may go untreated. Even with time off from work, a person's condition may become worse. In many cases, the only accessible source of medical care ends up being the emergency room, where care is very expensive.

Pregnancy and Job Loss

For women working in jobs with no medical insurance or provision for time off, a pregnancy may result in losing or leaving a job. Employers are not required by the federal government to pay their employees during maternity leave. Low-wage workers are often left with no choice but to work up until the last moment of their pregnancies and then leave their jobs. This is another factor contributing to the feminization of poverty.

THE IMPACT ON PUBLIC HEALTH

The health of workers in low-wage service jobs also affects the general public. As Beth Shulman wrote in *BusinessWeek*:

Without paid sick days, our public health suffers. Workers have no choice but to come to work sick and spread colds, the flu, and other ills to the public. In fact, the workers least likely to be provided paid sick days are those who prepare and serve our food, care for the elderly, look after our children, and help us in retail stores.[2]

But the impact of poverty on health goes beyond physical health. It can also impact an individual's mental health, which affects family relationships, work opportunities, and even survival.

Estelia Salvaron, an uninsured farmworker, harvests tomatoes in DiMare, Florida.

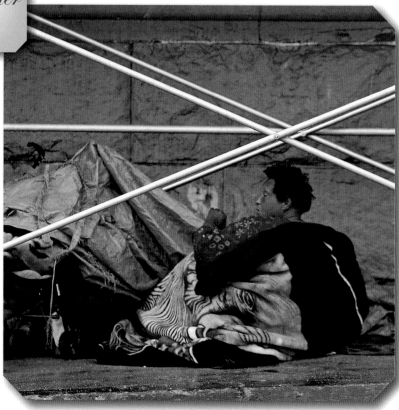

Homelessness is a last resort for many poor people who suffer from mental illness.

POVERTY AND MENTAL HEALTH

*M*ental health issues may not be obvious, but they are very real and have a long-term effect on poverty. In some cases, poverty is the result of mental illness, but poverty also causes mental illness. Either way, the two are closely linked.

The Mental Cost of Being Poor

In most developed countries, the highest rates of mental illness are found among poor people. The stress of living life in poverty frequently brings with it disorders such as depression and anxiety. People who do not have meaningful jobs with good pay often have low self-esteem. They may feel worthless, especially when the media makes it seem as though the rest of the world is well-off.

Constantly worrying about where the money will come from for the next rent payment or meal can bring on severe feelings of anxiety. Also, poverty brings about many stressful situations, including death, divorce, job loss, eviction, and illness. Poor people are more likely to be victims of violent crimes as well.

Studies have shown a link between levels of stress in families and their material well-being. During recessions, for example, increased job loss and poverty have been linked to a rise in violence in the home, including child abuse. Parents who are under stress from financial hardship may become unreasonable and intolerant. Their punishments may become excessive and severe, including demands backed by insults, threats, and physical abuse.

Parents may also feel guilty because they cannot spend quality time with their children. And children who do not receive enough parental attention may end up with low self-esteem and have trouble forming good relationships with other people. Those who spend much of their time in low-quality day care situations, which may be all that is available to low-income parents, may also have mental health issues.

The depression and anxiety that these children suffer will usually continue into adulthood.

LOOKING FOR ESCAPE

Substance abuse and dependence is a common mental health issue directly related to poverty. Poor people—especially teens— may look to drugs and alcohol as one

The Chicken-and-Egg Question

Researchers have known for many years that the lower a person's economic status, the more likely he or she is to suffer from some kind of mental disorder. But they have never been sure which came first—poverty or mental illness. Does poverty cause mental illness? Or does mental illness result in poverty?

New research is leaning toward a theory that poverty is more likely to come first. The stresses of poverty, such as unemployment and lack of a place to live, can increase the chance of having a mental illness. Some researchers even believe that living in relative poverty can influence one's psychological health. Continually comparing one's own circumstances to those of others can lead to dissatisfaction so extreme that it leads to mental illness, especially depression. Also, living in poverty can limit people's access to the kind of mental health services that would help control or treat their mental disorders.

way to escape from the stresses of poverty. Often, this initial impulse leads to addiction and substance abuse. Because it is legal and more affordable than other drugs, alcohol is often the drug of choice, and alcoholism is a common problem among the poor.

Other people may use more dangerous illegal drugs, such as heroin, cocaine, or methamphetamines. These expensive drugs lead already poor individuals even deeper into poverty. According to Darryl Chapman, a police officer:

> *The cocaine, marijuana and other types of drug dealers . . . search high and low for individuals that need a release from reality. Generally, those in need of an escape from their life the most are low income Americans. Once someone tries these drugs most of the time they become addicted and their lives turn even more south in need of more escaping from reality.*[1]

Those who use unclean needles to inject their drugs also risk infection, including AIDS.

Children and Mental Health

Children and youth from low-income households are more likely than their wealthier peers to suffer from mental health issues. According to a report from the National Center for Children in Poverty, 21 percent of low-income children ages 6 through 17 suffer from mental health problems. Of these children, 57 percent come from households with incomes at or below the poverty line. Many do not receive the services they need. As a result, they are more likely to end up in the juvenile justice system.

Through a program for people with mental disorders, Aron Washington has moved out of an institution and into his own apartment.

Addicts may also abuse certain kinds of prescription drugs, and many poverty-stricken people who receive prescription drugs through government programs may sell their medicines instead of taking them.

A Dangerous World

People living in poverty are often forced to live in unsafe neighborhoods, which pose another threat to their mental health. Crime and violence are common in the inner city. And people living in poverty may turn to crime. This may be because of their feelings of anger or desperation. It could also be from the need to get money for food, shelter, or drugs. Gangs and drug-trafficking activities put the entire neighborhood at constant risk of violence.

The possibility of injury or death to innocent people is very real, and is another cause of stress to people who live in poverty. Parents have the added burden of fearing for their children's safety. They may not allow their kids to play on the street or walk to schools or playgrounds. As a result, their children are deprived of playing outside and opportunities for exercise, which promote well-being.

FAMILIES AND POVERTY

Finally, poverty may have a negative effect on family structures. Many poor people live in single-parent or multigenerational homes, where the lack of two parents or overcrowded conditions adds stress. Because of crime, some family members may be in prison or in constant trouble with the police. Others might be involved in criminal activities that make family life more dangerous.

Single mothers are hardest hit by the lack of a second income and emotional support from another adult. According to researcher Ruby K. Payne, they also lack yet another valuable resource—a support system:

Relative Worth and Self-Worth

According to UNICEF, children who spend their lives living at an income level below their peers may suffer from long-term self-image issues. They will develop feelings of inadequacy and poor self-worth, which often leave them more vulnerable to abuse or exploitation.

A working definition of poverty is "the extent to which an individual does without resources." A support system is a resource. To whom does one go when help is needed? Those individuals available and who will help are resources. When the child is sick and you have to be at work—who takes care of the child? Where do you go when money is short and the baby needs medicine?[2]

Desperate single mothers, who have nowhere else to turn, may choose bad boyfriends or husbands who end up abusing their children. In turn, their children may end up without the nurturing, supportive role models they need to become healthy and successful adults.

Life can be a struggle for single mothers who support their families with low-paying jobs. Their circumstances may lead to homelessness.

The McNary family of Caldwell, Idaho, gathers for a meal. The family can no longer afford groceries for three meals a day.

THE SOCIAL ISSUES
OF POVERTY

Of all the effects of poverty, perhaps the most difficult for the poor to deal with are the social stigmas. In a world where the contrast between those who have and those who do not have is becoming increasingly apparent, society's attitudes

Poverty

can greatly affect poor people. Take the example of Katie and Sarah. Though they are fictional, their stories are based on real experiences:

Katie and Sarah are in the same classroom at their elementary school. Katie always has nice clothes and the latest toys and gadgets. She participates in nonschool activities such as gymnastics classes and music lessons, and she takes a vacation with her family to Florida every winter.

Sarah's mother is single and works two jobs to support Sarah and her sister. They live in a rented apartment. Sarah's clothes come from the consignment shop, she gets a free school lunch, and the only activities Sarah participates in are during school. As these two girls get older, the social gap between them will widen and become more and more obvious.

Class differences between the poor and rich begin showing up in elementary school. This is when disadvantaged kids may first realize they are living in poverty. Differences become even more apparent during the teen years, when possessions—the latest high-tech devices and even having a car—become more important. And media portrayals only reinforce the feeling of separation poor people may feel. On television shows, almost everyone seems to have a sufficient income to be comfortably upper middle class. When poor people are portrayed, they are usually cheerful and happy despite their economic conditions. Many middle-class people view poverty negatively, as a drain on their tax dollars—if they think about it at all.

The Invisible Poor

Many middle- or upper-class people do not often encounter the poor. Those who clean their offices, assemble their products, or package their food for minimum wages are not people they have relationships with. The wealthy might give money to charities that help the poor, but like everyone, they tend to socialize within their own social class. They do not usually befriend the people who receive their charity.

And when the wealthy do encounter the poor, they may not notice them. Streams of cars drive past a homeless person standing at an intersection. A minimum wage worker skips lunch because she cannot afford it, but her boss does not notice. Without experiencing it firsthand, poverty becomes abstract and distant, similar to a drought in Africa or the destruction of the rain forest. Writer James Fallows shared his experience with this phenomenon in the *New York Times Magazine:*

I often stayed late [at my office]. Around 9 p.m. I'd hear a knock on the office door. A woman in her [sixties], wearing a stiff-fabric vest with the logo of an office-cleaning company, stepped into the room to empty my wastebasket and collect Mountain Dew cans from the recycling bin. She walked as if her feet hurt. She did not have the bounce of the people I saw during the day. She kept making her rounds until about midnight. Eventually I started leaving the office to go home as soon as I heard her a few doors down. I was willing to read articles about the travails of the working poor. I just didn't want to watch her limp.[1]

Placing Blame

Only about 1 percent of federal tax money pays for welfare. And

Television Salaries

A person living in poverty may feel as though the rest of the world is far better off, especially if he or she watches much television. Characters seem to make enormous amounts of money no matter what they do, and they easily afford fancy cars and nice clothes. Such portrayals may not be very realistic. On the show *Desperate Housewives*, the character Susan Mayer is a children's book illustrator and a single mother. Still, she is able to afford a nice house. In real life, Susan would find difficulty making ends meet—even without the nice house.

yet controversy about the government program is intense. Some taxpayers argue that people on welfare need to take more personal responsibility. Some believe there are more effective ways of helping the poor. Still others resent that their tax dollars are begin spent to support others.

One consequence of the debate has been a social stigma regarding those on welfare. Welfare recipients may be perceived as lazy or unwilling to get jobs, even though many people who have jobs still require public assistance. Sar Levitan is an economist. He explained the contradictions in public opinion:

> We cannot for our own comfort let people starve and freeze on our streets, but we resent their accepting our largesse while indulging in counterproductive habits that we know would decrease our own productivity and well-being if we so indulged.[2]

People who rely on government assistance are sometimes seen as spoiled children who must be cared for despite their bad habits, and they do not seem properly appreciative. Some people believe welfare provides an easy living and that people remain on welfare on purpose.

Welfare recipient LaTanya Richardson of Kansas City, Missouri, looks for jobs online at an employment center.

POVERTY AND RACE

People of color in the United States experience lower incomes, higher rates of poverty, and shorter life spans than whites. In 2007, 24.5 percent of blacks, 21.5 percent of Hispanics, and 10.2 percent of Asians were poor. In comparison, 8.2 percent of non-Hispanic whites were poor. However, the actual number of white people living in poverty is more than that of people of color, simply because the white population is bigger.

Many white Americans share the mistaken belief that poverty only affects people of color. They may also believe that this is because of an individual's personal deficiencies. In reality, discrimination against these groups provides them with fewer opportunities for making a decent living. As the gap in wealth and income widens between whites and nonwhites, it becomes even more difficult for families of color to pull themselves out of poverty. This often results in the children living in poverty, which perpetuates generational poverty. For this reason, people belonging to minority groups have an especially difficult time coping with and escaping from poverty.

Immigrants from developing

The Extent of Disparity

A select group of white Americans were asked what they thought was the disparity in wealth between people of color and white people. This figure includes cash and possessions with monetary value, such as homes and cars. Most guessed relatively low amounts, such as $10,000. In reality, the color of a person's skin might mean having $150,000 less in wealth than a white family of a similar size. This study underscores a belief by researchers that white Americans underestimate the racial difference in wealth in the United States.

Race aside, the extent of disparity in general between the rich and the poor in U.S. society has been increasing since the late 1990s. In most of the nation, the incomes of wealthy people are rising more than twice as fast as the middle class. Even during the recession that began in 2008, the income gap widened.

countries may also become part of the invisible poor in the United States. Due to their inability to speak English or lack of education and training, they often end up in low-paying jobs, such as hotel maids or migrant farm laborers. In addition, many U.S. citizens resent immigrants—especially illegal ones—who come to their country and illegally receive welfare benefits. These citizens believe government assistance should be limited to native-born Americans.

The One with the Most Stuff Wins

Ultimately, a difficult aspect of living in poverty in a consumer-driven society such as the United States is the perpetual feeling of being left out. Advertising makes people believe that they need things that, in truth, are not at all necessary to their well-being or survival. In order to be happy, many Americans

The Middle Class

In good economic times, middle-class families make enough money to afford houses, cars, and some luxury items. However, they are also more likely to lose their jobs when the economy takes a turn for the worst. They suddenly find themselves without enough income to maintain their previous standard of living. In addition, they may be saddled with debt from expensive purchases or credit card loans that they accumulated in better times. As they fall into poverty, the gap between the very rich and the poor grows wider.

feel they must have the latest gadgets and trends in technology, fashion, decor, and so on.

For those living in poverty, the constant barrage of advertising and the examples of people who have what they want and need may make it difficult to maintain their positive self-images. As a result, they may make unwise decisions about spending. For example, a person might buy a wide-screen television when the money would be better spent on fixing a leaky roof or getting a more reliable car. Buying gives people material status. It helps them identify with others and makes them feel less invisible in society.

A shopper with a cart full of electronics symbolizes a consumer-driven culture in which a poor person may feel left out.

A volunteer sorts donated items at a food bank in Seattle, Washington.

ADDRESSING POVERTY

In developed countries, government programs provide health care, welfare for families, and social security for the elderly and the disabled. Most developing countries do not have similar programs. Poor people in those countries rely on international aid or simply do without any aid at all.

In developed countries, in addition to federal-level aid programs, many local governments work to combat poverty in their areas. Churches, religious groups, and other private organizations may also try to help, both locally and internationally. From food pantries to soup kitchens to homeless shelters, many types of aid attempt to limit poverty's negative effects.

In the United States

In the 1930s, the United States was struggling from a severe economic downturn. This era, called the Great Depression, was at its height in 1935, when the Social Security Act became law. Since then, the U.S. government has provided pensions for elderly people. This allows anyone over the age of 65 to receive a regular monthly check. The idea was that retired individuals who no longer earned income from regular jobs could use the pensions to support themselves.

Other forms of public assistance also were created. These included unemployment payments for people without jobs as well as money for families

with young or disabled children. The Social
Security Act signaled the beginning of the federal
government's philosophy that it was responsible for
the well-being of its citizens.

In the 1960s, this trend continued with the
Earned Income Tax Credit. This not only reduced
the amount of tax that workers with low incomes had
to pay, but it often gave them money back on the
taxes that had been withheld from their paychecks.

Most of these programs continue today. The
two best-known social insurance programs are
Social Security and Medicare, which provides health
care for the elderly and the disabled. In general,
eligibility for these programs is not based on
financial need.

On the other hand, public assistance programs,
such as welfare, are meant for low-income families.
Welfare may include cash payments and food stamps
for purchasing groceries. It may also provide in-kind
benefits. These noncash benefits include help with
housing, child care, school meals, and health care.

To qualify for help, a family's income must
fall below a certain level. Eligibility requirements
also include factors such as whether anyone in
the household is pregnant, disabled, ill, or has

a criminal conviction. They also take into consideration monthly household expenses, such as rent. The average payment for a family of four is approximately $500 in food stamps and $900 in cash per month.

In 1996, a movement began to put welfare recipients back to work and limit their dependence on governmental support. A new government program, called Temporary Assistance for Needy Families, stipulated a five-year limit for benefits. However, many people went from welfare to low-wage jobs. They could not pay for child care and other necessities and still required some form of public assistance.

GCAP

In 2005, many small anti-poverty groups joined forces to create Global Call to Action Against Poverty (GCAP). These groups included trade unions, community and religious groups, and organizations for women and youth. By forming an alliance, they hoped to pressure world leaders to end poverty and inequality. Among other things, GCAP is calling for trade equality, debt cancellation, and more aid for developing countries.

Myths about Welfare

Many negative myths unfairly portray welfare recipients. These myths include the idea that poverty comes from a lack of responsibility and being on welfare encourages people to be dependent. Other myths are that welfare promotes single mothers and births outside marriage and that it creates a culture of poverty that will be handed down through generations. Another misconception is that huge amounts of tax money support welfare, when it accounts for only about 1 percent of the federal budget.

Actual data disprove these myths. For example, from 1993 to 2002, the rate of single mothers participating in welfare programs actually decreased from 32 percent to 9 percent. At the same time, the number of people participating in work programs increased from 68 percent to 79 percent.

Some advocates for the poor argue that the myths promote bad public policy. These perceptions contributed to the welfare reforms of the 1990s, which they say were unsuccessful.

Other Programs for Combating Poverty

Some states attempt to reduce poverty by going after delinquent fathers who do not pay their court-mandated child support after a divorce. Many single-parent mothers and their children find themselves poverty-stricken after divorce, and by making these "deadbeat dads" fulfill their responsibilities, states hope to reduce that source of poverty.

Carolina Fuentes, right, waits with her daughter for an appointment at a Sacramento, California, welfare office.

Many secular and religious groups operate programs to alleviate poverty and hunger both in the United States and around the world. They include Save the Children, Bread for the World, Christian Children's Fund, and one of the most famous, UNICEF.

Coping with Poverty around the World

Such organizations provide aid to developing countries, while other organizations address their economic problems. The World Bank, the

Fair Trade

Bananas, chocolate, and other items are sometimes sold with a "fair trade" label. The label guarantees that the people in developing countries who harvested or produced the product received a fair wage. The fair trade movement works to alleviate poverty in poor countries.

International Monetary Fund (IMF), and the World Trade Organization try to negotiate fair trading terms for developing countries. They hope to improve economic growth by ensuring that countries receive fair prices for their goods. They also offer loans for projects to improve a country's infrastructure and provide jobs.

However, countries that have borrowed money from groups such as the IMF or the World Bank, or from developed countries, often find themselves saddled with debt. These countries are left with no additional money for programs that might reduce poverty. Heavily indebted poor countries such as Benin, Ethiopia, Ghana, Sierra Leone, Nepal, and Haiti have the highest levels of poverty in the world. They may owe more than four times the amount of money they make from exporting goods every year. Many are urging for debt relief by reducing or eliminating the crushing debt these countries owe. The hope is to free up money for essential programs such as health care and education.

Poor countries often rely on aid from wealthier nations. For the most part, however, the aid is not enough to even cover the debt payments going out. Most rich countries give far less than I percent of their total gross national income as aid to poor countries. Also, aid payments are not always put to good use and may end up going to corrupt leaders.

Finally, some developing countries have taken matters into their own hands. They have fostered grassroots movements where communities can undertake projects on their own to reduce poverty. For example, the government may issue a microcredit to a group of

Corruption in Zaire

Developing countries have huge debts in large part because of the corrupt practices of political leaders. These countries sometimes borrowed large amounts of money to spur development, only to have a dictator create even more debt, or worse, steal or squander the money. In 1980, Zaire (now the Democratic Republic of Congo) owed $5 billion to other countries. President Mobutu Sese Seko used much of that money while he was in office. Mobutu probably stole billions of dollars (the exact amount is unknown) before he was deposed and exiled from the country in 1997. He also had the profits from his country's diamond mines transferred to his own personal bank accounts overseas. Zaire's gross national product—the money generated by the country's industries and trade—was treated as a personal fund for Mobutu and his government. When he left, his country's debts had risen to $12 billion. Mobutu died in 1997, but his money is still being held in a Swiss bank. In 2009, the Democratic Republic of Congo was attempting to recover it through legal proceedings.

Millennium Development Goals

In 2000, the United Nations met and established eight Millennium Development Goals to be achieved by the year 2015:

1. End global poverty and hunger.
2. Provide universal education.
3. Promote equality for women.
4. Improve child health.
5. Improve maternal health.
6. Fight HIV and AIDS as well as other diseases.
7. Promote environmental sustainability.
8. Create a global partnership for development.

women. This is a small loan geared to people who have never been able to borrow money before. The women can establish a small business to sell their handcrafts and sewing.

In 2000, the United Nations outlined eight Millennium Development Goals to be completed by 2015. One of them was to eradicate extreme poverty worldwide. And yet, in 2009, one in two children in the world lived in poverty, and one billion people were illiterate. Many experts feel that eliminating poverty on a global level will never be possible. However, society has no choice but to strive to do so. As Frederick Douglass, an African-American abolitionist and author, noted more than 100 years ago:

Where justice is denied, where poverty is enforced, where ignorance prevails, and where any one class is made to feel that society is an organized conspiracy to oppress, rob and degrade them, neither persons nor property will be safe. [1]

*In Lagos, Nigeria, a boy urges the world to take action
on World Poverty Day, 2008.*

TIMELINE

1700 BCE

Hammurabi of Babylon creates laws for the treatment of the poor.

1601 CE

The Elizabethan Poor Laws are passed in Great Britain.

late 1700s

The Industrial Revolution begins in Britain; by the mid-1800s a new class of factory workers has been created in the West.

1932

Franklin Delano Roosevelt is elected U.S. president and begins to implement broad programs to combat unemployment.

1935

The U.S. Congress passes the Social Security Act.

1948

The Poor Laws in England end and are replaced with modern welfare programs.

1884

European countries divide up the land in Africa, each getting a slice of the "cake."

1914

Countries in Europe and North America control almost 90 percent of the world's land.

1929

After the stock market crash, the United States enters the Great Depression.

1948

The U.S. Congress votes to spend billions of dollars on aid to countries with widespread poverty as a result of World War II.

1980

The Brandt Report establishes the Brandt Line, defining rich and poor countries around the world.

TIMELINE

1996	1996	2000
The Heavily Indebted Poor Countries Initiative is created to cut the debt of the world's poorest countries.	The U.S. welfare system undergoes reforms through the Personal Responsibility and Work Opportunity Reconciliation Act.	The United Nations establishes eight Millennium Development Goals, which include ending global poverty and hunger.

2005	2005	2007
Large parts of debt owed by one-third of the world's poorest countries are forgiven.	Global Call to Action Against Poverty is organized.	The rate of poverty in the United States is 12.5 percent; the poverty line for a family of four is $21,203.

2003	2004	2005
Conflict begins in Darfur, causing widespread famine and genocide.	The growth of fair trade coffee imports to the United States has grown 75 percent since 1998.	Twenty-six percent of people worldwide live in poverty.

2008	2009	2009
The United States begins suffering from an economic recession, resulting in more people living below the poverty line.	The movie *Slumdog Millionaire,* which portrays poverty in Mumbai, India, wins eight Academy Awards.	One in two children in the world lives in poverty.

ESSENTIAL FACTS

AT ISSUE

❖ In 2005, 26 percent of people worldwide lived in poverty. In 2007, the rate of poverty in the United States was 12.5 percent.

❖ In the United States, poverty disproportionately affects people of color.

❖ Societies have blamed and punished the poor, but they have also aided and protected them. In the United States, the idea that the federal government was responsible for society's poor came about under President Franklin Delano Roosevelt in the 1930s.

❖ Colonization put in motion great discrepancies between Western countries and developing countries.

❖ Poverty can be caused by a multitude of factors. In developing countries, these include overpopulation, subsistence farming methods, environmental problems, war, racism, lack of education, lack of trade, corrupt or ineffectual government, and unequal distribution of resources worldwide.

❖ The effects of poverty in the United States include homelessness, poor education, and poor physical and mental health. These factors also cause poverty, creating a vicious cycle.

❖ Poverty also creates a social stigma in the United States. The poor are often invisible in a consumer-driven society.

❖ Myths about welfare include that the program is expensive or encourages recipients to stay dependents of the state, but data disprove this idea.

❖ Poor countries saddled with debt rely on Western countries, the World Bank, and the IMF for help. However, aid given does not begin to meet the need.

❖ Poverty affects all of society in a number of ways, including crime rates, taxes, school quality, and public health.

CRITICAL DATES

Late 1700s
The Industrial Revolution began in Great Britain, leading to a new class of factory workers.

1884
European countries divided up land in Africa, cementing the colonial structures that have caused poverty in that continent.

1933
President Roosevelt began transforming the role of government in the U.S. economy.

2000
The United Nations made the goal of ending global poverty by 2015.

QUOTE

"Poverty is acute distress: The lunch that consists of Doritos or hot dog rolls, leading to faintness before the end of the shift. The 'home' that is also a car or van. The illness or injury that must be 'worked through,' with gritted teeth, because there's no sick pay or health insurance and the loss of one day's pay will mean no groceries for the next. These experiences are . . . by almost any standard of subsistence, emergency situations. And that is how we should see the poverty of so many millions of low-wage Americans— as a state of emergency." —*Barbara Ehrenreich in* Nickel and Dimed: On (Not) Getting By in America.

ADDITIONAL RESOURCES

SELECT BIBLIOGRAPHY

"Causes of Poverty." *Global Issues.* 2009. <http://www.globalissues. org/issue/2/causes-of-poverty>.

"Data and Research." *The World Bank.* 2009. <http://econ. worldbank.org/WBSITE/EXTERNAL/EXTDEC/0,,menuPK:476 823~pagePK:64165236~piPK:64165141~theSitePK:469372,00. html>.

Ehrenreich, Barbara. *Nickel and Dimed: On (Not) Getting By in America.* New York, NY: Henry Holt, 2001.

Iceland, John. *Poverty in America: A Handbook.* Berkeley, CA: University of California Press, 2003.

Payne, Ruby K. *A Framework for Understanding Poverty,* 3rd edition. Highlands, TX: aha! Process, Inc., 2003.

Smith, Billy G., ed. *Down and Out in Early America.* University Park, PA: The Pennsylvania State University Press, 2004.

FURTHER READING

Haugen, David M., ed. *Social Issues Firsthand: Poverty.* Farmington Hills, MI: Greenhaven, 2005.

Kamberg, Mary-Lane. *Bono: Fighting World Hunger and Poverty.* New York, NY: Rosen, 2008.

Obadina, Tunde. *Africa: Progress & Problems: Poverty and Economic Issues.* Broomall, PA: Mason Crest, 2006.

Senker, Cath. *What If We Do Nothing? Poverty.* Milwaukee, WI: World Almanac Library, 2007.

WEB LINKS

To learn more about poverty, visit ABDO Publishing Company online at **www.abdopublishing.com**. Web sites about poverty are featured on our Book Links page. These links are routinely monitored and updated to provide the most current information available.

FOR MORE INFORMATION

For more information on this subject, contact or visit the following organizations.

Franklin D. Roosevelt Presidential Library and Museum
4079 Albany Post Road, Hyde Park, NY 12538
800-FDR-VISIT
www.fdrlibrary.marist.edu/index.html
The library has displays about the Great Depression and Roosevelt's role as president at that time.

Local Food Banks
Local phone books list food banks and pantries where donations are gladly accepted and volunteers may be needed to help sort food. Feeding America's Web site, http://feedingamerica.org, features a "food bank locator."

Local Salvation Army Branch
www.salvationarmyusa.org/usn/www_usn_2.nsf
Local Salvation Army branches are located throughout the United States. They have thrift stores where purchases raise money to help the needy. Many also run soup kitchens and homeless shelters. Visit the Salvation Army online to find the nearest branch.

Glossary

absolute poverty
The condition of not having enough of the basics for survival, such as food, clothing, and shelter.

colonization
The practice of a country or people having control over another country and its resources.

depression
A period of time with widespread unemployment, declining values in the stock market, and low levels of business activity. Depression is also a mental disorder marked especially by extreme sadness and inactivity.

desertification
The process by which an area of formerly fertile land becomes a desert.

developed country
A country, such as the United States, that is one of the richest in the world, with highly industrialized farming, high levels of literacy, and social services for the poor.

developing country
A poor country, one marked by low industrialization, high rates of illiteracy, and few, if any, services for the poor.

famine
Widespread hunger.

genocide
The deliberate extermination of a racial, national, cultural, or political group.

gentrification
The result of a large-scale move to buy and renovate run-down properties in low-income areas and make them attractive to high-income buyers, thereby displacing low-income families.

immigrant
A person who migrates, or moves, to another country.

industrialization
  The process of introducing industry to an area or a society on a large scale.

malnutrition
  Poor health as a result of not having enough food or food of proper quality.

poverty line
  The level of annual income below which a household is said to be living in poverty.

recession
  A period of economic downturn, not as severe or as long-lasting as a depression.

relative poverty
  The condition of being poor in comparison to most other people living in a society.

resources
  Money, assets, or mental support that can be drawn on in a time of need; also the collective wealth of a country or its means for producing wealth.

Social Security
  A U.S. government program whereby retired people receive monthly payments to help make ends meet.

subsistence farming
  Farming that provides enough for a farm family to survive with little extra for sale.

transitional country
  A country involved in a shift from one government to another.

welfare
  A system in which the government collects tax money and uses it to provide aid for those who need it.

Source Notes

Chapter 1. What Is Poverty?

1. "In Pictures: Voices from Ethiopia's Looming Famine." *BBC News Online*. <http://news.bbc.co.uk/1/shared/spl/hi/pop_ups/03/africa_voices_from_ethiopia0s_looming_famine>.

2. Barbara Ehrenreich. *Nickel and Dimed: On (Not) Getting By in America*. New York: Henry Holt, 2001. 214.

Chapter 2. A History of Poverty

1. Norman H. Murdoch. "King Leopold's Ghost: A Story of Greed, Terror, and Heroism in Colonial Africa." *Journal of Third World Studies*. Fall 2002. 9 May 2009 <http://findarticles.com/p/articles/mi_qa3821/is_200210/ai_n9115146/>.

Chapter 3. Poverty Today

1. Charlie LeDuff. "Detroit Teenager Dreams of Escaping Poverty." *The Detroit News*. 7 June 2008. 9 May 2009 <http://www.detnews.com/apps/pbcs.dll/article?AID=/20080607/METRO/806070339>.

2. Ibid.

3. Charlayne Hunter-Gault. "Land Ownership Elusive for South Africa's Poor." *National Public Radio*. 14 Feb. 2009. 9 May 2009 <http://www.npr.org/templates/story/story.php?storyId=5624419>.

4. John Schenk. "Not Enough Winter Shoes to Go Around in a Typical Kosovar Family." *World Vision*. 16 Apr. 2004. 9 May 2009 <http://meero.worldvision.org/news_article.php?newsID=429>.

Chapter 4. The Underlying Causes
1. "World Poverty Stories: Child Labor in Africa: Ghana." *Cozay.* 2009. 9 May 2009 <http://cozay.com/WORLD-POVERTY-STORIES.php>.
2. "Poverty and Inequality." *Share the World's Resources.* 2009. 9 May 2009 <http://www.stwr.org/poverty-inequality/>.
3. Fact Sheet. *Institute for Women's Policy Research.* 27 Oct. 2008. 9 May 2009 <http://www.iwpr.org/pdf/C350_8.2008.pdf>.

Chapter 5. Homelessness
1. "Homeless, Poor Freeze in US Cold Wave." *World Socialist Web Site.* 5 Feb. 2003. 9 May 2009 <http://www.wsws.org/articles/2003/feb2003/cold-f05.shtml>.
2. "Fact Sheet and Lesson Plan for Sixth-Eighth Grade Students." *National Coalition for the Homeless.* 2009. 9 May 2009 <http://www.nationalhomeless.org/publications/facts/Fact%20Sheet%20and%20LessonPlan-6-8.pdf>.
3. "NCH Fact Sheet #1: Why Are People Homeless?" *National Coalition for the Homeless.* 2009. 9 May 2009 <http://www.nationalhomeless.org/publications/facts/Why.pdf>.
4. Bea Sheftel. "Homeless Living in Cars." *Suite101.com.* 21 Nov. 2001. 9 May 2009 <http://www.suite101.com/print_article.cfm/homelessness/85858>.

Source Notes Continued

Chapter 6. Poverty and Education

1. Ruby K. Payne. *A Framework for Understanding Poverty*, 3rd ed. Highlands, TX: aha! Process, Inc., 2003. 23.

2. William L. Bainbridge and Thomas J. Lasley II. "Poverty, Not Race, Holds Back Urban Students." *Columbus Dispatch*. July 2002. 9 May 2009 <http://www.schoolmatch.com/articles/poverty.htm>.

Chapter 7. Poverty and Health

1. Ruby K. Payne. *A Framework for Understanding Poverty*, 3rd ed. Highlands, TX: aha! Process, Inc., 2003. 34.

2. Beth Shulman. "Make Paid Sick Days Universal: Pro: Flu Sufferers Belong in Bed, Not in the Cafeteria." *Business Week*. Dec. 2008. 9 May 2009 <http://www.businessweek.com/debateroom/archives/2008/12/make_paid_sick.html>.

Chapter 8. Poverty and Mental Health

1. Darryl Chapman. "Poverty and Drug Abuse: Does One Lead to the Other?" *Policelink.com*. 2007. 9 May 2009 <http://www.policelink.com/training/articles/3186-poverty-and-drug-abuse>.

2. Ruby K. Payne. *A Framework for Understanding Poverty*, 3rd ed. Highlands, TX: aha! Process, Inc., 2003. 17.

Chapter 9. The Social Issues of Poverty
1. James Fallows. "The Invisible Poor." *The New York Times Magazine*. 19 Mar. 2000. 9 May 2009 <http://www.nytimes.com/2000/03/19/magazine/the-invisible-poor.html>.
2. John Iceland. *Poverty in America: A Handbook*. Berkeley, CA: University of California Press, 2003. 118.

Chapter 10. Addressing Poverty
1. Frederick Douglass. *BrainyQuote*. 2009. 9 May 2009 <http://www.brainyquote.com/quotes/authors/f/frederick_douglass_2.html>.

INDEX

ABOUT THE AUTHOR

Marcia Amidon Lusted has written more than 20 books for young readers, as well as numerous magazine articles. She is an assistant editor for Cobblestone Publishing and an instructor for the Institute of Children's Literature. She lives in New Hampshire with her family.

PHOTO CREDITS

George Rhodes/AP Images, cover; Ric Francis/AP Images, 6; Anita Powell/AP Images, 9, 98 (top); Jorge Saenz/AP Images, 13; North Wind Picture Archives, 14, 96; Getty Images, 21, 97 (top); Damian Dovarganes/AP Images, 22, 68; Pat Roque/AP Images, 26; Vadim Ghirda/AP Images, 29; AP Images, 30; Eugene Hoshiko/AP Images, 36; Mark Duncan/AP Images, 39; Mel Evans/ AP Images, 40, 97 (bottom); Red Line Editorial, 44; Ed Kashi/ Corbis, 49; David Richard/AP Images, 50; Nick Ut/AP Images, 54; Rich Pedroncelli/AP Images, 59; Chris Knight/AP Images, 60; Eric Draper/AP Images, 63, 99; Ed Kashi/Corbis, 67; M. Spencer Green/AP Images, 72; Michael Barley/Corbis, 75; Matt Cilley/AP Images, 76; Charlie Riedel/AP Images, 81; Joe Imel/AP Images, 85; Elaine Thompson/AP Images, 86, 98 (bottom); Rich Pedroncelli/AP Images, 91; Sunday Alamba/AP Images, 95